THE NATURE OF
WALRUSES

PETER KNUDTSON

THE NATURE OF
WALRUSES

WHITE-TUSKED

WANDERERS

OF THE SEA

GREYSTONE BOOKS
Douglas & McIntyre
Vancouver/Toronto

PAGES II–III

The vast majority of the world's walruses are seasonal wanderers, following the southern margins of Arctic sea ice as it advances and retreats. FRITZ PÖLKING/ PETER ARNOLD, INC.

PAGE IV

A big bull walrus strikes a pose. Its immense size, long tusks, massive neck and shoulders, and wrinkled hide indicate that it is fully grown. LEONARD LEE RUE III

PAGE VIII

Walruses congregate on the beach at Round Island, Alaska. RANDY BRANDON/PETER ARNOLD, INC.

98 99 00 01 02 5 4 3 2 1

Greystone Books
A division of Douglas & McIntyre
1615 Venables Street
Vancouver, British Columbia
V5L 2H1

Originated by Greystone Books and published simultaneously in the United States of America by Sierra Club Books, San Francisco.

CANADIAN CATALOGUING IN PUBLICATION DATA
Knudston, Peter.
The nature of walruses

ISBN 1-55054-621-X

1. Walruses. 2. Walruses—Pictorial works. I. Title.
QL737.P62K68 1998   599.79'9   C98-910024-3

The quotations in the text are from the following sources. Full bibliographical information is given in the Selected References.
Page 7: from *Through the Looking Glass, and What Alice Found There* by Lewis Carroll, pp. 75–76; page 15: from *The World of the Walrus* by Richard Perry, p. 4; page 67: from *The World of the Walrus* by Richard Perry, p. 32; page 84: from *The Pinnipeds: Seals, Sea Lions, and Walruses* by Marianne Riedman, p. 57; page 87: from *Across Arctic America* by Knud Rasmussen, p. 151; page 90: from *The World of the Walrus* by Richard Perry, p. 116.

Editing by Nancy Flight
Jacket and text design by Isabelle Swiderski
Front jacket photograph by Mats Forsberg
Back jacket photograph by Bryan and Cherry Alexander

Printed and bound in Hong Kong by C & C Offset Printing Co., Ltd.

The publisher gratefully acknowledges the assistance of the Canada Council and of the British Columbia Ministry of Tourism, Small Business and Culture. The publisher also acknowledges the financial support of the Government of Canada through the Book Publishing Industry Development Program for its publishing activities.

One of the most remarkable creatures in the Arctic is the walrus (Odobenus rosmarus)*, whose very existence and natural history were cloaked in mysticism and anthropomorphism until the 19th century.*

——FRANCIS FAY, "The Ecology and Biology of the Pacific Walrus"

CONTENTS

PREFACE

This book is an introductory exploration, through words and images, of the natural history of the walrus. In researching and writing this book, I have approached my elusive subject not from the perspective of a seasoned walrus researcher but rather as a nature writer and biologist who, a quarter of a century ago, carried out modest studies of the social behaviour of harbor seals off the coast of northern California. Consequently, my narrative is drawn almost exclusively from the available historical, ethnographic and scientific literature on the walrus, supplemented by occasional observations of captive animals—not from vast personal field experience.

Given the formidable geographical and environmental challenges inherent in studying walruses in the wild, only a handful of zoologists around the world can claim to be bona fide experts in walrus biology and behaviour. And I have necessarily relied heavily on published accounts of their patient, often heroic field observations.

I would like to express, once again, my indebtedness to those biologists whose reports are cited in the pages that follow. And I would be remiss if I did not single out the contributions of the late Francis Fay, a lifelong champion of walruses, friend of the Inuit and the foremost American authority on the Pacific walrus in this century.

I want to express my deep gratitude to Nancy Flight, editorial director of Greystone Books, and an old friend, for her exceptional patience, dedication and expertise in guiding our third book project together to publication. In addition, my thanks to Rob Sanders for his continued support, as well as for suggesting my topic, and to fellow nature writer Candace Savage for her thoughtful editorial advice.

I would also like to thank Gerald W. Garner, a wildlife biologist in the Biological Resources Division of U.S. Department of the Interior, Anchorage,

Alaska, for generously agreeing to review my manuscript for scientific accuracy, as well as Isabelle Swiderski for her fine book design and Leanne Denis for her exhaustive photo research.

Finally, I salute the many wildlife photographers whose handsome and hard-won images of walruses in wild settings breathe life into this book in ways that words alone could not possibly hope to.

PAGES XII–XIII

A herd of walruses bathed in Arctic sunlight. THOMAS KITCHIN/FIRST LIGHT

THE WONDER

Part One

OF WALRUSES

Bloodshot eyes glared solemnly from its wrinkled face, as ugly as a gargoyle's.
Formidable, gleaming white tusks curved down from the corners of its upper
lip, which was further embellished by [bristly whiskers]. At every movement
of its immense bulk heavy folds of rust-brown hide undulated curiously.

—RICHARD PERRY, *The World of the Walrus*

Aesthetic speculation aside, it is clear to the most untutored eye that the walrus
was not designed for beauty. It is, plainly put, one of the homeliest creatures
ever to grace the planet.

—SARA GODWIN, *Seals*

OF BEAUTY AND BEASTS

A huge walrus, adrift on an Arctic ice floe off the coast of Alaska, the paired white
spikes of its ivory tusks contrasting with the cinnamon-brown of its thick, rumpled,
sparsely haired skin, surely ranks as one of the most remarkable and improbable
spectacles in all of nature. But for most of us, who are unlikely to visit the distant
Arctic shores and ice fields that are the walrus's home, it is also likely to remain
one of nature's rarest sights.

The walrus, along with the wolf, whale, lion, tiger, elephant and a few other
elite wild animals around the world, is a true animal icon, a member of that select
bestiary that has loomed large in human consciousness from the beginning of time.
Even if we have never laid eyes on a great, white-tusked walrus basking beneath

FACING PAGE

Walruses are extraordinarily
sociable animals. They live
and travel in herds that vary in
size and composition throughout
the year. ART WOLFE

THE WALRUS

REMAINS, IN MANY

WAYS, A MODERN

BIOLOGICAL ENIGMA, A

GHOSTLY APPARITION

OUT ON ARCTIC

SEASHORES AND

RESTLESS ICE FLOES.

the midnight Arctic sun, few of us have difficulty in conjuring up such a scene, drawing on the cultural images of this species that reside in the collective mind's eye of Western civilization.

Why do we, however fleetingly, care about the walrus (if not the real walrus in the natural world, then at least the animal caricature that inhabits our imaginations)? What has drawn human beings, over the ages and across vast geographic distances, in fact and in fiction, in art as well as in science, to this ungainly, comical and even grotesque sea mammal? What singular qualities of biological "beauty," adaptability and grace do the more fervent walrus fans see in this bizarre, blubbery, buck-toothed beast? What in its peculiar physical appearance, anatomical architecture, behavioural repertoire and ecological niche have so superbly equipped it to flourish for millions of years in an evolutionary theatre of frigid, wind-lashed northern seas and fearsome winter storms? And what, in the end, are the terms of our often uneasy bond with his species—past, present and future?

Our current understanding of walruses is largely fragmentary, anecdotal and confused. For one thing, most of the world's walruses live in the exceedingly remote, icy vastness of the circumpolar Arctic seas, often far removed from the curious gaze of even the most indefatigable research scientist. For another thing, walruses spend the bulk of their lives immersed in water and all but hidden from our view.

Even when walruses do leave the sea to rest on terrestrial hauling grounds, many animals prefer isolated, drifting ice floes to more accessible (to us) island or mainland shores. Nor do walrus breeding rookeries, to the limited extent that biologists have studied them, bear much resemblance to the classic, densely packed "cities of seals" so typical of more familiar, highly territorial pinnipeds such as fur seals or sea lions. Rather, walrus populations are often widely dispersed out on the vast open sea ice during the dark, blustery winter breeding season. As a result, many of the intimacies of their ordinary social lives are all but invisible to most human observers. For all these reasons, the walrus remains, in many ways, a modern biological enigma, a ghostly apparition out on Arctic seashores and restless ice floes.

FABULOUS WALRUSES

Considering the magnitude of our ignorance, it is perhaps not surprising to learn that human perceptions of walruses over the millennia have often been littered with gross exaggerations and misconceptions, as well as shards of truth. To date, no historian has yet compiled a thorough chronology of humanity's kaleidoscopic images of walruses over the centuries, comparable to those that exist, for example, for whales and wolves. But even a brief sampling of the images of this species in history, art and literature reveals humankind's sense of awe and wonder about— as well as revulsion for—this remarkable sea mammal.

In the sixteenth century, for instance, in their monumental treatises on exotic animals around the world, leading European naturalists often portrayed walruses, whales, seals and other seldom encountered marine mammals as fabulous, often nightmarish, dragonlike monsters of the sea. A few openly portrayed walruses as ferocious, man-eating beasts of prey. For example, in his scholarly writings, Olaus Magnus, a leading sixteenth-century Swedish clergyman, described walruses living along the coast of Norway as "Great Fish as big as Elephants" that would, if they chanced to encounter a tasty human strolling along their shores, promptly attack and "rend him with their Teeth."

Occasionally, however, European images of walruses during this era are not quite so easy to divine. In 1521, the famous German painter and engraver Albrecht Dürer, renowned for his detailed, visionary paintings of biblical scenes, made a simple pen-and-ink drawing of a walrus. Although Dürer's wildlife

In the midst of a herd, a mother walrus nuzzles her young calf. ANONYMOUS

drawings were widely admired, this one was perhaps somewhat compromised by the fact that his subject turned out to be a single pickled walrus head that he was allowed to briefly sketch while it was in transit as a gift to Pope Leo X from a Catholic bishop.

To Dürer and most of his contemporaries, walruses could only have been viewed as extraordinarily exotic creatures, comparable perhaps to our images today of a duck-billed platypus or a spiny anteater. What mysterious gleam, one is tempted to ask, did the master artist perceive in the clouded eyes of this deceased walrus? Did its lifeless form provide Dürer with a sort of blank canvas on which he might reveal some faint trace of his culture's accumulated fantasies about this rare beast?

We cannot be sure. For the animal depicted in Dürer's painting is (perhaps not surprisingly, considering the less than ideal circumstances of this portrait "sitting") unnaturally withered, contorted and gaunt. The only hint of the diabolical in the strange, scrawny, sabre-toothed creature that gazes out at us is that it is slightly wild-eyed and its nostrils seem flared.

Still, few would dispute humankind's tendency to project its own deep, often perverse psychological needs on fellow life-forms, a process that has been amply documented in our troubled relationships with, for instance, wolves, whales, sharks and snakes, among other creatures. In the case of the walrus, the record is similar but far more scanty and sporadic. In Europe, as elsewhere, fabulous notions about walruses have never entirely disappeared. In most cases, popular notions about walruses were never written down. They were simply transmitted by word of mouth as local anecdotes, experiences or gossip. In the nineteenth century, for example, when a wayward Arctic walrus occasionally strayed far south of the polar pack ice into British waters, Victorian sailors might picturesquely describe the rarely sighted sea mammal as "unearthly and demoniacal."

But sometimes such walrus lore did find its way into the tapestry of recorded literature. For instance, generations of children have been initiated into some of the mystical and mysterious aspects of popular Western views of walruses through Lewis Caroll's beloved nineteenth-century fairy tale, *Through the Looking Glass*.

Carroll's fictional walrus, appearing in the whimsical children's verse titled *The Walrus and the Carpenter,* is certainly no ordinary walrus. In fact, he is a slightly diabolical humanoid figure: a street-smart con man, who sports long tusks resembling the drooping handlebar mustache of a sly London barroom

Lewis Carroll's famous fairy-tale characters the Walrus and the Carpenter. ORIGINAL DRAWING BY JOHN TENNIEL, IN *Through the Looking Glass* BY LEWIS CARROLL dandy. And he is inclined to speak in perplexing puns and riddles, as in this familiar quote, issued just before he devours four unsuspecting young Oysters:

> "The time has come," the Walrus said,
> "To talk of many things:
> Of shoes—and ships—and sealing wax—
> Of cabbages—and kings—
> And why the sea is boiling hot—
> And whether pigs have wings."

Carroll's preposterous animal figure is also torn by decidedly conflicting emotions. For only after gorging on the tender flesh of four sentient oysters that he and the Carpenter have duped does this savvy sea mammal pause to express belated remorse for his murderous misdeeds. Handkerchief to bloodshot walrus eyes, the conniving pinniped apologizes profusely to his innocent bivalve victims for having so thoughtlessly devoured them, sobbing, not quite convincingly, "I weep for you. I deeply sympathize."

The walrus as mirror to some of our deepest human hopes, fears and longings has even made a fleeting appearance in the lyrics of modern pop music. To cite just one example: in the 1960s, in the same land and almost exactly a century after the publication of Caroll's classic children's book, the Beatles crooned a tune on their legendary, highly successful *Magical Mystery Tour* album enigmatically entitled "I am the Walrus."

Penned by the wickedly witty late John Lennon, its lyrics, narrated by a slightly surreal walrus, feature a hallucinatory cascade of strange images and sounds, ranging from existential "egg men" to watery gurgling noises presumably intended to evoke a walrus's underwater world.

I won't pretend to have deciphered Lennon's motives for composing a pop song steeped in pinniped paranoias (although you can be certain the topic was earnestly debated in countless college dormitories a few decades ago). But some observers have characterized Lennon's apocalyptic walrus as a mythical animal voice from the dim and fluid depths of the human unconscious. One music critic, somewhat grandly yet in all seriousness, went so far as to suggest that the upstart Beatles, knowingly or not, had invoked the walrus as a symbol of their own subconscious yearnings for identity and order in their increasingly chaotic times. At the very least, Lennon's lyrics do present a twentieth-century image of the walrus that is as dark, mysterious and even demonic as Carroll's better-known one penned a century earlier.

WALRUSES IN THE WILD

So what do we know about walruses? Even if you have never seen a living walrus, you can probably conjure up a brief laundry list of at least some of this animal's key physical characteristics.

There is, for example, the walrus's prodigious size. In fact, among pinnipeds, the clan of fin-footed sea mammals that includes seals, sea lions and walruses, only the gargantuan elephant seal is larger. The average mature Pacific walrus male, for example, weighs approximately 1200 kilograms (2650 pounds) and measures a bit more than 3 metres (10 feet) long. The average adult female weighs about 800 kilograms (almost 1800 pounds) and measures 2.6 metres (8.5 feet). Thus, bulls, which must aggressively compete for females during breeding season, weigh, on average, fully 50 per cent more than cows.

There are the walrus's distinctive, long ivory tusks. (No other living pinniped possesses them.) Walrus tusks are actually enormously elongated upper canine teeth, deeply embedded in the animal's thick skull and protruding beneath the upper lip. Tusks are found in both adult males and females, grow throughout life and can reach lengths of up to a metre (3 feet) in bulls and .6 metre (2 feet) in cows.

Like an elephant's tusks, they are valuable weapons against potential intruders of all shapes and sizes. But they also serve as important visual signals of an individual walrus's age, sex or social stature and are routinely brandished or used to poke opponents during squabbles among herd members. As you shall see, they probably play a minor role in certain forms of bottom-feeding behaviour. And, as mentioned, they may also, on occasion, be used as ambulatory aids, something like ice axes, when a walrus scrambles over particularly slippery or treacherous terrain.

This novel "tooth-walking" function of tusks caught the attention of many early walrus watchers, as can be seen, for example, in this passage by Olaus Magnus:

A walrus's muzzle is covered with hundreds of stiff, quill-like whiskers. A walrus uses this bristly mustache to nuzzle other walruses, grub for shellfish on the muddy seafloor and even grasp food and other objects. JOE MCDONALD

They will raise themselves with their Teeth

as by Ladders

to the very Tops of the Rocks,

that they may feed on the Dewie Grass,

or fresh Water,

and roll themselves in it,

and then go to the Sea again,

unless in the meanwhile they fall very fast asleep,

and rest upon the Rocks.

If you have watched walruses in a zoo or on a TV wildlife documentary, you may be able to recall a few other characteristic physical features of the walrus. Among them: the walrus's blunt, rounded head, which is rather small in comparison with its large torso; its tiny, bulging, often bloodshot eyes; and its rounded tongue tip. Other distinctive features include its broad, boxy muzzle, bristling with stiff, straw-coloured whiskers, or mustachial vibrissae; its lack of external ear flaps; its massive neck and chest musculature; and its powerful webbed flippers. Besides its tusks, perhaps the most distinctive characteristic of the walrus is its wrinkled expanse of loose, nearly naked skin (generally darker and hairier in young walruses), which gives this beast the almost cartoonish appearance of a playful toddler dressed up in oversized adult clothing.

Some wildlife aficionados might even be able to dredge up a few examples of typical walrus behaviour. For example, like many other pinnipeds, walruses tend to be extremely sociable, hauling out, or resting, on ice or land in dense herds that can be as tightly packed as rush-hour commuter trains in New York City. Less well known is that unlike many of their mostly fish-eating pinniped kin, walruses feed predominantly on benthic, or bottom-dwelling, marine shellfish such as clams.

FACING PAGE

A walrus uses its mobile whiskers almost as fingers to tactually explore or even pick up objects. It sometimes also erects them as a gesture of submission to a more dominant herd member.

GEORG BANGJORD

But beyond these facts, most of us might confess that we really know remarkably little about this odd-looking and geographically isolated marine mammal, whose entire existence is virtually circumscribed by the Arctic Circle. For the walruses of the world are exclusively Arctic animals; they all frequent shallow areas of the Arctic Ocean and adjoining seas. There is, in short, no such thing as an "Antarctic" walrus.

All living walruses belong to a single species: *Odobenus rosmarus*. The first—or generic—name, *Odobenus*, is derived from Greek terms meaning "tooth walker" or "one who walks on his teeth." The name has its origins in early observations of walruses using their upper canine teeth, or tusks, to help hoist their bulky bodies out of the water, climb up rocky slopes or scramble over slippery ice. The second—

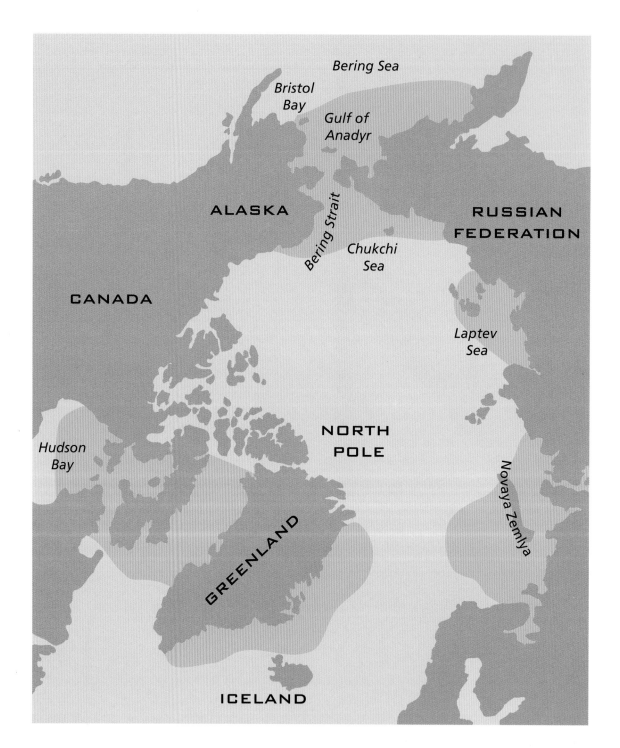

Bering Sea

Bristol Bay

Gulf of Anadyr

ALASKA

Bering Strait

RUSSIAN FEDERATION

Chukchi Sea

CANADA

Laptev Sea

NORTH POLE

Hudson Bay

Novaya Zemlya

GREENLAND

ICELAND

PURPLE AREAS
INDICATE THE
WORLD GEO-
GRAPHIC RANGE
OF THE WALRUS
*Adapted from Sara
Godwin,* Seals, *p. 93*
(Polar view)

or specific—name, *rosmarus,* is derived from an assortment of Scandinavian names for the walrus, including *rosval, rosm* and *haval.*

The term *walrus* itself has roots in a rich soil of archaic linguistic terms, a number of which make reference to a "whale horse," "sea horse" or "sea cow." Because the walrus has historically inhabited vast regions of the circumpolar Arctic, it is familiar to people the world over. In Swedish, for example, the walrus is called *hvalross;* in Icelandic, *hross-hvalr;* in Old English, *horsch-wael.* Modern Russians refer to the walrus as *morzh;* the French call it *morse;* Germans know it as *walross.* The Inuit know it as *aivuk* or *aivik.*

Today most scientists recognize two distinct subspecies of living walruses: the Pacific walrus and the Atlantic walrus. The Pacific walrus, *Odobenus rosmarus divergens,* is larger and vastly more numerous than its Atlantic counterpart. First recognized as a separate subspecies in 1815, it frequents the Bering and Chukchi Seas, ranging from the northeastern coast of Siberia to the northwestern coast of Alaska. Today the single largest seasonal concentration of Pacific walruses often occurs near Wrangell Island in the Chukchi Sea. There is also a small subpopulation of several thousand walruses centred in the Laptev Sea off the Siberian coast that some scientists have suggested should be considered a third subspecies.

The Atlantic walrus *(Odobenus rosmarus rosmarus)* is found in the eastern Canadian Arctic, especially the northern reaches of Hudson Bay, as well as along the coasts of Greenland and Ellesmere Island. Farther to the east, it also occurs in small, scattered populations in the vicinity of, for example, Bear Island, the Spitzbergen Islands and various other remote islands to the north of Norway, and on Franz Josef Land and Novaya Zemlya off the northern coast of Russia.

The two subspecies can be separated on the basis of several distinctive, but relatively minor, physical differences. For example, the Pacific walrus, when full grown, is larger than its Atlantic cousin. It also has somewhat longer tusks, which,

PAGES 20–21

Framed in ice, an Atlantic walrus loafs on an ice floe near Southampton Island in Canada's Northwest Territories.
NORBERT ROSING

19

as its subspecies name suggests, may bow or diverge. Its nostrils are slightly higher on its muzzle. And its body coloration tends to be somewhat darker.

No accurate census of the world's total population of walruses exists. Over the past several decades, Pacific walrus populations are thought to have recovered considerably from earlier drastic declines, which resulted from centuries of human exploitation. The total number of Pacific walruses today, according to recent estimates, probably exceeds 200,000 animals. Since Atlantic walrus populations are so much smaller and more widely dispersed, estimates of their total numbers tend to be even more speculative. And in many areas, they simply have not yet fully recovered from centuries of devastation by humans. Today their numbers are measured in mere thousands.

An Atlantic walrus can be distinguished from its Pacific cousin by its smaller body, narrower skull and shorter tusks. WAYNE LYNCH

Early walruses

Where did walruses come from, and how does modern evolutionary science explain their current distribution in the Arctic?

It is impossible to even begin to grasp the extraordinary scientific creation story of walruses without first reviewing a few essential facts about the evolutionary roots of the whole pinniped clan. All of the seals, sea lions and walruses in the world belong to a large clan of kindred amphibious "fin-footed" marine mammals known as the Pinnipedia. Shaped by evolutionary forces both on land and in the sea, they share a host of biological and behavioural similarities. But their streamlined contours, webbed limbs and aquatic ways often cloak deeper differences, suggesting that pinnipeds arose from more than one ancestral group of terrestrial mammals.

Most scientists believe that the pinniped family tree has three principal branches. The first branch, the so-called true seals, is made up of such familiar species as the harbor seal, the harp seal and the elephant seal, among others. The members of this branch are thought to have descended from ancient, land-based, otterlike ancestors that inhabited coastal North Atlantic waters during the Miocene epoch, perhaps 20 million years ago or more. Sea lions and walruses comprise the other two branches. They appear to be more closely related to each other than to true seals and probably arose from terrestrial, bearlike ancestors inhabiting the margins of ancient North Pacific seas.

The earliest ancestors of the modern walrus lived primarily along northern coastal areas of the Pacific Ocean. These primordial walruses first appear in the fossil record during the early Miocene epoch, about 15 million years ago. At this time, the northern Pacific basin offered a rich and largely unexploited source of food for proto-pinnipeds, including ancestral walruses.

The walrus branch of the great pinniped tree gradually radiated into a number of different walrus twigs, or genera. Each newly emergent form of proto-walrus

OF THE PACIFIC

OCEAN. THESE

PRIMORDIAL

WALRUSES FIRST

APPEAR IN THE

FOSSIL RECORD

DURING THE EARLY

MIOCENE EPOCH,

ABOUT 15 MILLION

YEARS AGO.

developed its own unique evolutionary adaptations to its particular surroundings. Among them: specialized tooth structures, food preferences, swimming abilities, diving capacities and assorted other biological traits. In the process, some mobile members of the modern walrus's family came to inhabit Pacific waters as far south as California and Mexico.

Then a momentous change occurred. By the late Miocene, perhaps 9 to 10 million years ago, the principal arena of walrus evolution began to shift from the Pacific to the Atlantic Ocean. First, small numbers of walruses inadvertently wandered from their natal Pacific waters into the Atlantic via a natural sea passage through the isthmus of Central America, which had recently formed as a result of global climate changes and rising seas. Those migrants that survived the transoceanic swim were rewarded with access to a vast, virtually untapped source of marine food in a distant ocean that had never before known walruses.

But this gateway to the Atlantic did not remain open long. Approximately 5 million years ago, decreasing global temperatures and declining sea levels reversed the process, closing the trans-Central American sea corridor to the Atlantic, thereby geographically separating Atlantic and Pacific walrus populations. Then the walrus lineage began to suffer a series of stunning extinctions throughout much of its now transoceanic range. Oddly enough, the only walruses that survived this brief flurry of extinctions turned out to live in Atlantic waters. And all of these survivors belonged to the single genus *Odobenus*, the same one to which all modern walruses belong today. In time, the descendants of these survivors would range as far south as France in the eastern Atlantic Ocean and as far south as South Carolina in the western Atlantic. Meanwhile, the immense Pacific Ocean, the evolutionary birthplace of the ancient walrus lineage, was left utterly bereft of walruses.

But the story does not end here. Before the last great glacial age (and possibly as recently as seventy-thousand years ago), small numbers of walruses—members,

PAGES 28–29
A herd of Pacific walruses huddle together, creating a geometric jumble of gleaming white tusks. TOM AND PAT LEESON

27

by now, of the single modern species—gradually began to make their way back to recolonize northern Pacific waters. This time they took a northern route. Over many generations, they travelled through transient, climatically induced cracks in the great sheets of Arctic sea ice that had previously formed a solid, impenetrable barrier to such forays.

The evolutionary history of walruses had come full circle. To summarize, from their ancient beginnings in the North Pacific, early ancestors of modern walruses had first slowly fanned out to inhabit vast areas not only of the Pacific Ocean but also eventually of the Atlantic Ocean. Later, waves of chance extinctions gradually eliminated walruses from Pacific waters, leaving behind only relic *Odobenus* populations in the Atlantic region. Then, perhaps seventy-thousand years ago (a mere blink of the eye in geologic time), generations of modern walruses, descendants of these hardy Atlantic survivors, began to swim back through newly available northern sea channels to gradually repopulate the walrus-less northern Pacific. Finally, when these northern corridors in the Arctic pack ice once again refroze, Pacific and Atlantic walrus populations, no longer able to freely interbreed, proceeded to evolve independently in splendid geographic isolation—a continent apart—and they have continued to do so to this day.

FACING PAGE

Walruses can live to at least forty years of age. Because most cows give birth in alternate years, population growth can be ponderously slow. WAYNE LYNCH

PAGES 32–33

Like ghostly apparitions, a herd of walruses rests in the fog. THOMAS KITCHIN

THE WAYS

Part Two

OF WALRUSES

Sometimes the water seemed actually alive with them, so closely packed were their great bodies. In their haste to get away they lunged over each other, coughing and grunting, rising high in the water, sinking down, endlessly rolling about, as they swung their great flippers through the brine.

—C.M. SUTTON, Canadian zoologist, from field notes describing
a herd of fleeing walruses near Southampton Island,
Hudson Bay, "The Mammals of Southampton Island"

SHAPED BY THE SEA

On land, the walrus is an awkward, lumbering giant, a belching, quivering mountain of flesh, bone and blubber, all draped in loose folds of pale skin, a sea mammal built like a Japanese sumo wrestler. Yet the instant it plunges into water, its true home, it is somehow instantly transformed into a creature of extraordinary athleticism and grace as it glides silently, effortlessly under water, with all of the innate elegance of a great soaring bird in flight.

To make sense of this paradox, we must turn to evolutionary biology. Natural selection has engineered the bodies of walruses for both an aquatic and a terrestrial existence. Walruses spend an estimated two-thirds of their long lives immersed in frigid Arctic waters. Most of the remaining third is spent

FACING PAGE

In a whirlwind of spray, two Pacific walrus bulls engage in a fierce aquatic fight off Round Island, Alaska. Similar battles take place between breeding bulls out on remote Bering Sea breeding grounds in the darkness of winter. JEFF FOOTT

35

loafing on hauling grounds, on ice or land, where they are often exposed to even more severe environmental conditions, including ferocious sea storms and huge swings in temperature.

Because ancestral walruses emerged from ancient stocks of terrestrial mammals, many key features of walrus anatomy and physiology are modifications of a basic terrestrial body plan.

Pinnipeds, including walruses, evolved an array of physical features that made their bodies smoother and more streamlined, permitting them to glide gracefully through the water with minimal turbulence. They developed sleek, torpedo-shaped bodies. Their heads gradually became rounder, smoother and more bullet shaped. Hair or fur became sleek, close cropped or even (as in today's virtually naked adult male walruses) vestigial. External ear flaps and other bodily protuberances were gradually reduced or eliminated. A male walrus's genitals became fully retractable, withdrawing like a plane's landing gear inside smooth body contours to reduce unnecessary drag. Finally, a thick capsule of cutaneous fat, or blubber, provided additional hydrodynamic padding, as well as providing vital insulation and serving as a seasonal food storage depot.

Evolution has also elegantly retooled ancient land mammal limbs to meet the new task of swimming in water. The assortment of elegant, oarlike flippers found in all seals, sea lions and walruses arose from the same skeletal structures that had once stiffened the legs of swift terrestrial ancestors. Thus, the bones of a walrus's foreflipper are made up of modified land mammal limb bones: fingers, hand, wrist and a portion of forearm. (A walrus's arm pit, however, unlike our own, forms at about the middle of the forearm bone.) Similarly, a walrus's hindflipper is made up of mammalian toe, foot and ankle bones, all neatly encased in a smooth, elastic casing of skin. The larger bones of the leg are buried, out of sight, inside the external body wall.

A Pacific walrus heaves its immense body ashore. Walruses sometimes use their tusks to haul themselves onto an ice floe or over slippery rocks.

FRED BRUEMMER

A WALRUS IN MOTION

As an amphibious mammal, a walrus is capable of locomotion both on land and in the water. But, like other pinnipeds, it is awkward, even ungainly out of water. Like kindred sea lions and fur seals, it lumbers along on land on foreflippers and hindflippers, which are folded forward at the ankle joint beneath its body. (In contrast, a harbor seal or other true seal scoots along without the aid of its hindflippers, which trail limply behind it.) And the skin covering the bottoms of its flippers has a rubbery, almost warty texture, providing traction on slippery ice or rock.

On land, a walrus's huge body is so heavy that its flippers alone ordinarily cannot bear the full weight of its massive head and torso. So a walrus carries a portion of this immense burden on its broad ventral surface. It moves forward on

37

land using a combination of slapping foreflipper and hindflipper strides and lurching, caterpillarlike movements on its belly. As strange as it may sound, a terrestrial walrus lumbers along, strictly speaking, on its wrists, hands, ankles and feet (not just on its "palms" or "soles"), and on its broad belly.

Only under water does the walrus's gargantuan form reveal its true grace. Buoyed up by water, its great bulk is no longer flattened, as it is on land, by the unforgiving forces of gravity. And its stubby limbs are no longer forced to strain under its staggering body weight. It seems to glide through the water almost effortlessly, using its paddle-shaped hands and feet, each equipped with fingers and toes that are webbed like a scuba diver's flippers.

As it swims, a walrus often relies largely on its hindflippers for propulsion. Alternately, each fanlike hind limb thrusts laterally towards the main axis of the body. Massive muscles in the lower body power each stroke, causing the animal's lower abdomen to sway rhythmically from side to side like a dancer's.

Unlike sea lions, walruses do not routinely "fly" like a bird through the water with their foreflippers. Rather, they tend to use their short, squarish forelimbs far more sparingly. At times, the foreflippers provide thrust in the form of quick breast strokes. But ordinarily they act more as rudders, steering the animal during acrobatic twists, turns and tumblings, fuelled by the undulating hindflippers.

Diving deep

Walruses are bottom-feeders, dining largely on marine mollusks, echinoderms, annelids and other benthic organisms that dwell on shallow ocean floors throughout their range. Unlike many pinnipeds, they do not routinely prey on fish or other swift-moving marine organisms. So speed is generally not a top priority; they are strong but relatively slow swimmers, rarely exceeding about 7 kilometres (4.3 miles) per hour. Nonetheless, if disturbed, a fleeing walrus can reportedly surge and snort for short distances through surface waters at speeds of up to 35 kilometres (22 miles) per hour.

The benthic marine organisms that make up the bulk of a walrus's diet tend to be concentrated at depths of less than 90 metres (300 feet). So routine feeding dives seldom need to last longer than about ten minutes. Still, walruses have been known to dive to depths of at least 113 metres (370 feet) and remain under water for as long as twenty-five minutes, and they are almost certainly capable of exceeding such impressive aquatic feats.

How do they do it? First, walruses are anatomically equipped to withstand the extreme pressures of deep ocean dives. A walrus's valvelike nostrils and ear openings shut tightly, forming a waterproof plug. Its ear tubes contain special tissues that help equalize differences in pressure between inner and outer ear chambers. And its rib cage is partially collapsible, thereby forcing surplus air out of the lungs and minimizing the perils of potentially lethal blood-gas disorders, such as the bends.

Second, a walrus's circulatory system is evolutionarily equipped to ensure efficient storage, transport and utilization of oxygen during prolonged periods under water. Pinnipeds typically have a much larger volume of blood in relation to the size of their bodies than do comparably sized terrestrial mammals (blood comprises about 12 per cent of pinniped body weight, compared with about 7 per cent in humans, for example). In addition, their red blood cells are relatively large and are laden with oxygen-loving hemoglobin molecules (enabling a Weddell seal,

FACING PAGE

Walruses spend nearly two-thirds of their lives in the water. And it is in the icy depths of Arctic seas that many of the most crucial events of their life cycle, including feeding, courtship and mating, take place.
ERWIN AND PEGGY BAUER

for example, to store up to five times the quantity of oxygen per blood volume in a human being). Blood vessels are modified to increase blood storage capacity. And muscle tissues possess elevated levels of myoglobin, another molecule that preferentially binds with and stores oxygen, providing these animals with yet another auxiliary reservoir of oxygen for use during prolonged dives.

The walrus's circulatory system has a host of other remarkable features to aid diving. It automatically shunts scarce oxygen-laden blood to such key organs as the brain, heart and lungs during dives, thereby maintaining the animal's consciousness and vital body processes at all costs. At the same time, it automatically reduces blood flow to peripheral regions of the body. In so doing, it conserves finite stores of oxygen by temporarily depriving skin, viscera, flippers and other body parts of oxygen, without causing permanent tissue damage.

Walruses also drastically lower their heart rates during deep dives. This built-in physiological process, known as bradycardia, permits the animal to stretch oxygen reserves even further. In concert with other circulatory mechanisms, a reduced heart rate also diminishes the volume of blood coursing through restricted pathways during dives without triggering sudden life-threatening drops in blood pressure. When a fatigued animal resurfaces, its heart rate quickly soars, rapidly replenishing the body's myriad oxygen depots.

Walruses even possess special anatomical features that help them catch their breath and even rest for a time in choppy Arctic seas. Adults are outfitted with special expandable throat regions known as pharyngeal pouches. These membranous sacs tend to be larger and more elaborate in breeding bulls, where they seem to serve as natural resonating chambers, amplifying their strange, bell-like courtship vocalizations.

But the pharyngeal pouches serve another equally useful function; like old-fashioned Mae West life preservers, when inflated, they form a buoyant collar, allowing a bone-weary walrus to float, even sleep, almost effortlessly in an upright position at sea.

Heat and cold

Cool, dense sea water robs warm mammalian bodies of heat far more rapidly than air does. To cope with heat loss, walruses have large bodies. As a result, there is less surface (skin) area in relation to the walrus's mass (the inside of the body), minimizing dissipation of body heat through exposed skin.

Adult walruses are virtually naked, with no more than a sparse covering of bristly hairs (although newborn and young walruses do temporarily sport much denser coats of hair, which presumably provide some insulation to their smaller, more vulnerable bodies). As a result, unlike some of their relatives, they have come to rely almost exclusively on blubber, dense insulating layers of cutaneous fat tissue, to help retain precious body heat.

Blubber is far from perfect as an insulator. In fact, it may be less effective than dry hair in certain terrestrial situations. But it does release heat less rapidly than other connective tissues in the body. And, equally important, when a walrus dives into the ocean depths, its rippling layers of body fat are not as compressible as fur tends to be and therefore are likely to retain more of their original insulating value.

Walrus blubber conserves heat largely by serving as a blanket of insulation. And, with the onset of the Arctic winter, it will expand to a thickness of up to 15 centimetres (6 inches). Because blubber is richly vascularized with networks of fine capillaries, it is also capable of releasing surplus heat—in much the same way that a car radiator does—during warm summer days on the hauling grounds. Here is how it works. If an adult walrus is basking on ice or land during the annual hormonally induced shedding of hair and skin known as the summer molt, its body automatically diverts the blood flow to vessels located in and around its cloak of blubber. As the fat-laden outer capsule of the body becomes temporarily engorged with warm blood, surface capillaries dilate, releasing excess body heat to surroundings.

This heat-reducing mechanism can lead to startling colour changes in a hauled-out summer herd of basking walruses. For in the process of dilating its surface capillaries, a dozing adult walrus's ordinarily pallid skin gradually turns a bright shade of pink in a full-body blush.

PAGES 44–45

Overheated walruses turn pink as dilated capillaries in their skin become engorged with blood. RANDY BRANDON/ PETER ARNOLD, INC.

WALRUSES MAY SLIP INTO THE WATER,

SWIM UNDER A FROZEN CHANNEL AND

SMASH THROUGH ACCUMULATED

LAYERS OF ICE

OVERHEAD, USING

THEIR MASSIVE

SKULLS AS SLEDGE-

HAMMERS AND

STRIKING REPEATED

BLOWS.

SEASONS OF THE PACIFIC WALRUS

Walruses are seasonal wanderers. Extraordinarily social mammals, they live and travel in herds that vary in size and composition throughout the year, faithfully following, for the most part, the southern margins of the Arctic sea ice during its cyclic oscillations between summer and winter latitudes.

The annual movements of the Pacific walrus are far better known than those of its sparser and more geographically dispersed Atlantic cousin. In winter, Pacific walruses are usually found along the southernmost edge of the open pack ice that forms a vast frozen sheet over much of the Bering Sea. In the eastern Pacific region, they are concentrated in an area bounded roughly by St. Lawrence Island, in the northern Bering Sea, and Bristol Bay, along the southwestern shores of mainland Alaska. In western Pacific waters, they are centred on the Gulf of Anadyr, along the Siberian coast of Russia.

During these months of ferocious storms and endless polar nights, densely packed herds of resting walruses huddle together against the cold along natural fractures, or leads, in the pack ice. These breaks form intricate networks of channels in the sea ice that provide vital escape routes to the sea for the ever vigilant animals as they rest. And they also offer easy access to shallow waters during routine feeding excursions.

Sometimes the winter wind chill factor becomes extreme, causing physical discomfort or even threatening the very survival of herds out on these wind-whipped hauling grounds. At such times, individual walruses may occasionally abandon the highly exposed ice floes in favour of the calmer and relatively warm sanctuary of adjacent seas. Here they will rhythmically dive, surface and rest near the ice floes until the weather improves, immersed in an undersea world tinted in seemingly infinite shades of blue.

In Arctic winters, temperatures can plummet, sometimes causing leads to quickly freeze over and placing entire herds in peril. Not surprisingly, nature has amply equipped the walrus to cope with such life-threatening contingencies.

Walruses may, for example, slip into the water, swim under a frozen channel and smash through accumulated layers of ice overhead, using their massive skulls as sledgehammers and striking repeated blows. A walrus can reportedly break through ice over 20 centimetres (8 inches) thick using nothing more than its hard head. Alternatively, walruses may use their tusks as ice picks to laboriously chip away at the edges of small breathing holes, thereby maintaining vital access to two worlds.

In about April, as the spring calving season begins, the main herds of Pacific walruses begin their long, arduous journey north to the nutrient-rich waters of the Chukchi Sea. This immense body of water stretches from the mouth of the Kolyma River on the eastern Siberian coast to Point Barrow, Alaska.

Walruses are hardly the only participants in this extraordinary annual animal exodus; they are joined by a synchrony of other returning Arctic life-forms. As this vast Noah's Ark of animal migrants heads north, each species proceeds at its own pace. Eventually, though, they are forced to funnel through the narrow Bering Strait. This results in an extraordinary, if fleeting, seasonal concentration of Arctic animal life as skies overhead darken with dense clouds of seabirds and waterfowl in flight and seas churn with passing flotillas of walruses, seals, whales and other sea mammals. Because they tend to be slow but strong and persistent swimmers, the migrating walruses often augment their daily progress by hitching rides on ice floes conveniently adrift on northerly currents.

Eventually, the Bering Strait opens into the Chukchi Sea. Here the walruses, by now in the company of hordes of fat new calves born during the arduous northern journey, feed ravenously all summer long on this marine ecosystem's enormous seasonal pulses of marine invertebrate populations. This rich diet allows each walrus

to grow rapidly and lay down considerable body fat, resulting, by season's end, in a thick robe of blubber that will later help sustain the animal in the less productive surroundings of the southerly Bering Sea wintering grounds.

In summer, as at other times of the year, these main herds of Pacific walruses tend to remain close to the fractured southern fringe of polar sea ice. Broken into floating rafts, these great, groaning white plains of ice offer a number of advantages over alternative land-based refuges.

First, because each platform of ice extends far out into the open sea, it provides loafing walruses with ready access to areas of shallow ocean floor that might otherwise be all but inaccessible to them. Second, because it is anchorless and adrift, it grants herds access to a constantly shifting seafloor landscape of tasty clams, whelks and other marine shellfish. And third, its remoteness from the mainland provides resting herds of walruses with a measure of freedom from predators and other potential disturbances.

Despite such benefits, these herds do, on occasion, abandon the thinning summer pack ice, particularly during very warm summers, in favour of more secure hauling grounds on nearby island or mainland shores. Here, on land as on ice floe, they will squabble interminably, shed skin and hair, digest bloated bellyfuls of seafood and fitfully sleep.

The precise social structure of the northern herds remains uncertain. Out on the northern summer feeding grounds, most Pacific walrus herds appear to be maternal herds, made up largely of adult females and their young of both sexes and various ages, including recently born calves. But there are also reports of scattered all-male groups, as well as occasional groups containing adults of both sexes in some locations.

The vast majority of male Pacific walruses, including both adults and subadults, do not appear to take part in the great northern sea trek to the Chukchi Sea at all. Rather, tens of thousands of them spend the summer in densely packed all-male herds located in more southerly coastal regions of this species' range.

These exclusively male herds can be spotted, for example, on traditional terrestrial hauling grounds in Bristol Bay, off the southwestern coast of Alaska, as well as in the Gulf of Anadyr, along the eastern Siberian coast.

Interestingly, these groups do not appear to be the classic bachelor herds of nonbreeding male "outcasts" encountered in sea lions, fur seals and other pinniped species. Rather, most of these males are actually fully grown, sexually mature bulls—animals in their prime that are not reproductive rejects at all but rather have already mated during the previous winter out on the Bering Sea breeding grounds. For the duration of the brief Arctic summer, these noisy congregations of males will, like the main herds in the Chukchi Sea, spend most of their time on land bickering, molting and dozing in the sun, segregated, during these months of seasonal gluttony, from the rest of the population located far to the north.

In the fall, the northern summer herds of Pacific walruses begin to head back south on the return leg on their long annual journey. Fattened by months of gorging, they make their way once again through the narrow pincers of the Bering Strait, joined, as in spring, by great seasonal throngs of other migrating birds and sea mammals.

As before, the walruses swim as well as ride on ice floes. And again, they travel, as if prodded by the icy fingers of the advancing Arctic winter, just ahead of the slowly expanding southern margin of the pack ice.

By December, most of these animals are back in their traditional winter areas of the Bering Sea. Soon they are joined by thousands of bulls that have just completed less arduous trips north from their more southerly summer refuges along the Alaskan and Siberian coasts. The returning herds appear to converge in two principal Bering Sea regions—near St. Lawrence Island, just south of the Bering Strait, and in the general vicinity of Bristol Bay, well off the southwestern coast of Alaska, as well as in the Gulf of Anadyr, and it is in these regions that the reunited populations will spend the winter.

By this time, huge sheets of sea ice have gradually glazed over much of the

Bering Sea, forcing the herds of overwintering walruses to huddle together against the bitter cold along in the southern margins of the ice. Out on the desolate, windy ice fields, shrouded in the near darkness of Arctic winter, sexually mature members of the population will begin to mate.

Breeding typically takes place between December and March, usually peaking in February and March, long before winter storms have relaxed their icy grip on these remote hauling grounds. Here, in an ancient reproductive ritual that has assured the continuity of their kind for millennia, thousands of bulls and cows in the winter herds court, consort and copulate, far from the prying eyes of all but the most dedicated human walrus watchers.

Eventually, when spring once again gradually unfolds and the pack ice begins to break up, the great northward exodus of the population's main herds will begin all over again. In obedience to the Arctic's rhythm of alternately retreating and advancing sea ice, the main walrus herds, made up largely of adult and subadult females and young animals, will once again travel 3000 kilometres (nearly 2000 miles) or more in their marathon trip from the Bering Sea to the Chukchi Sea and back again. Meanwhile, groups composed exclusively of males will once again separate from these main herds and fan out to the southeast and southwest to congregate in the summer male herds out on their own traditional summer feeding grounds along the coasts of Alaska and Siberia.

It is an impressive journey. Taken in its entirety, the Pacific walrus's annual migration ranks with some of the longest and most arduous migrations of other sea mammals.

TAKEN IN ITS ENTIRETY, THE PACIFIC WALRUS'S ANNUAL MIGRATION RANKS WITH SOME OF THE LONGEST AND MOST ARDUOUS MIGRATIONS OF OTHER SEA MAMMALS.

SEASONS OF THE ATLANTIC WALRUS

The annual movements of scattered Atlantic walrus populations are often far less well documented than those of Pacific walruses. Evidence suggests, however, that the annual movements of the small concentrations of Atlantic walruses found in Hudson Strait and the northern part of Hudson Bay and Foxe Basin, for instance, tend to be rather local and restricted. And Atlantic walrus populations living off the coasts of Greenland, Baffin Island, Franz Josef Land and other areas each appear to follow their own respective seasonal migratory path. In at least some parts of their vast range, Atlantic walruses probably do not migrate at all, choosing instead to linger in one place throughout the year as permanent local residents.

Like their Pacific counterparts, those Atlantic walrus populations that do migrate tend to follow the southern boundaries of the polar sea ice. Each spring, following the annual breakup of local pack ice, they, too, often travel to traditional summer feeding grounds, where they feed on their favourite marine invertebrate species that thrive on the floor of plankton-rich seas under a blazing Arctic sun. And they often form sexually segregated herds during the summer. In the fall, they will also abandon these fertile waters, just ahead of the advancing Arctic pack ice, to return to warmer, more hospitable waters where populations recongregate for the winter and breed.

Not every migrating walrus takes part in the return leg of the journey. For reasons unknown, small numbers of both Atlantic and Pacific walruses choose to stay in frigid northern latitudes for the duration of the Arctic winter. Against all odds, as the winter pack ice slowly tightens its noose around them, some of these hardy animals manage to survive by staying close to stretches of open ocean, called polynyas, that remain free of ice year round or by clinging to smaller ice-free zones formed by fast-flowing marine currents.

WALRUS SOCIETY

*Threat displays are
usually enough to settle
most dominance disputes.
But should they fail, bouts
can quickly escalate into
full-blown, often bloody
battles.* JEFF FOOTT

Scientists have much to learn about the social lives of walruses in wild settings.
Only a few decades ago, for example, most marine mammalogists thought that the
Pacific walrus probably mated in late spring or early summer, close to the same
time that pregnant cows gave birth to their calves, rather than, as we now know,
in the dark months of northern midwinter. And only quite recently have biologists
even begun to decipher the the intimate secrets of walrus society. But until biologists
have made year-round studies of individually identified animals, we must make do
with little more than tantalizing clues.

In now appears that during the breeding season the fittest bull walruses stake
out and defend small, often fluid aquatic breeding sites that are close to herds of cows

58

hauled out on the winter pack ice. Males hotly contest the limited quotas of aquatic space in order to secure these sites, which have been called pinniped variations of a lek, condemning less dominant bulls to more peripheral hauling areas.

A classic lek is a specialized form of breeding territory observed in birds such as grouse and hoofed mammals such as the Uganda kob during the height of the reproductive season. Typically, each dominant male in the group occupies and defends its own tiny terrestrial arena, in which he carries out elaborate courtship displays in order to try to attract the attention of sexually receptive females nearby.

A bull walrus's breeding site is, however, not so neatly partitioned as the leks of male grouse or Uganda kob. Subject to the endless vagaries of shifting ice floes and fickle female herds, the boundaries of the watery breeding arenas of amorous bull walruses appear to be constantly in flux and are far less rigid and predictable than the terrestrial leks of many other species.

A Pacific walrus bull's flamboyant courtship activities take place both above and below water. When the bull is submerged, he makes special stereotyped courtship calls, each one often lasting several minutes or more. Some researchers have compared these strange, pulsing "songs" to the sounds of distant bells ringing. Their eerie metallic quality probably arises, in part, from the acoustic effects of the large, elastic pair of pharyngeal pouches in the bull's throat, which serve as natural resonating chambers. These distinctive bell-like tones are typically followed by a series of loud knocking sounds. When the bull surfaces, he routinely emits a series of short, harsh whistling sounds or sharp, staccato "clacking" noises, the latter created by the rapid, teeth-chattering vibrations of his jaws.

Simultaneously, scores of competing bulls, each spaced 10 metres (30 feet) or so from his nearest neighbour and in plain view of the resting cows, carry out similar stereotyped courtship behaviours. The overall effect of this riotous visual and acoustic courtship activity has been compared to the "wolf whistles" and other

As a pair of Pacific walruses
duel, a lone horned puffin
momentarily alights amid
cinnamon-brown mounds of
blubber that probably look
disconcertingly like boulders.
HENRY H. HOLDSWORTH/
WILD BY NATURE

expressions of unbridled human machismo one might expect to encounter in a Friday night gaggle of rowdy teenage boys.

Each walrus bull courts nearby groups of resting females with a passion. In time, a female responds to the displays of her assembled suitors by exiting the herd to approach the male of her choice. Whether she chooses her mate on the basis of his masculine charms or his prime real estate holdings is not known for certain. Before long, the pair engages in intimate bouts of mutual nuzzling, sexual play and diving. Actual copulation is thought to take place under water (although it may occasionally occur on the pack ice) facilitated by the male's extraordinarily long (up to 62 centimetres, or 24 inches) baculum, or penis bone, the largest of any living mammal. Most likely mating occurs as the pair indulges in graceful, tandem nuptial dives beneath the sea.

Pacific walrus society is polygynous. This means that each dominant bull routinely mates with a number of female partners. In an unmistakable sign of polygynous social structure, cows out on the pack ice at the height of the breeding season outnumber bulls by a ratio of between 5:1 and 15:1. After each brief union, a bull abandons his mate and begins to court a new partner, until he has eventually bred with a succession of cows. His numerous romantic liaisons all take place in or near the tiny, hard-won patch of aquatic real estate that constitutes his individual breeding site.

Dominant bulls do not generally tolerate the presence of adult or subadult males in their aquatic breeding arenas. So, in addition to their courtship and mating duties, they must also vigilantly patrol the boundaries of their breeding sites. When a bull encounters another male, he typically tries to intimidate the intruder by holding his great tusks in a highly visible, raised horizontal position, a standard threat display among walruses. He may also make loud, aggressive chattering sounds that have been compared to the sound of a hammer banging on a metal pipe.

If the intruder fails to promptly retreat in the face of such threats, the interaction can quickly escalate. The two combatants may, for example, engage in a series of bluff charges or bouts of lightning-quick parries and thrusts of their sabrelike tusks, punctuated by resonant growls or deep, throaty leonine roars.

In most cases, the outcome of such a dispute tends to be fairly predictable: the bigger, stronger bull that is outfitted with the more dazzling pair of tusks generally wins. This result helps explain why males are so much larger than females in this species as well as in other polygynous pinniped species.

The vast majority of disputes between breeding bulls (as well as between other walruses) are resolved before either animal suffers a potentially life-threatening injury. Nonetheless, battles between bulls do, on occasion, escalate to full-blown fights. It is not uncommon, for example, for a bull's thick, knobby, amourlike chest, neck or shoulder skin to become stained with blood flowing from fresh puncture wounds or lacerations inflicted by an agile opponent. But more often than not, threat gestures and calls will suffice. And sometimes, as if in a final parting display of walrus bravado, a victorious bull will, just as a vanquished male is retreating to less perilous waters, signal his triumph with defiantly raised tusks.

MOTHER AND CALF

The walrus's breeding system is built on a reproductive cycle that is, in some ways, unique among pinnipeds. The walrus possesses the lowest known reproductive rate of any pinniped species, with cows generally bearing no more than a single calf every two to three years, a fact that has serious implications for the long-term survival of walruses in the wild.

Why is the walrus's birth rate so low? First, walruses are relatively long-lived creatures, with a life span in the wild that can exceed forty years, and they are notoriously late bloomers. Pacific walrus males, for example, tend to become sexually mature around the age of ten, females around the age of eight. Moreover, the majority of male walruses do not seem to actively participate in courtship and mating until they are closer to fifteen, and females may not give birth for the first time until they are nearly ten.

Second, the bond between a walrus mother and her calf is extraordinarily long and intimate. Following birth, a mother nurses and stays close to her offspring for between 2 and 2½ years, longer than in any other pinniped species. During this prolonged and socially intense relationship—one of the strongest maternal bonds among all mammals—she and her demanding offspring are likely to remain virtually constant companions. Since females tend to stay in the same herd, this relationship may continue into adulthood for female calves. Most young males will eventually join all-male herds.

When her calf grows weary, the mother will routinely carry the young animal piggyback as she swims. Or if she suddenly perceives danger, she may even clutch the calf to her breast with her foreflippers as she dives, in a manner that astonished observers over the centuries have openly compared to a human mother protectively cradling her infant.

A walrus calf typically weighs between about 40 and 65 kilograms (between about 90 and 140 pounds) at birth, and it grows rapidly on a diet of fat-rich milk (approximately 30 per cent of the milk is fat) that it consumes greedily during sporadic nursing bouts carried out on ice and at sea. On an ice floe, a mother may nurse her calf in typical pinniped fashion by exposing her retractable teats as she lies on one side. But more commonly she nurses her young at sea.

At such times, the pair is sometimes compelled to assume almost comically contorted postures. For example, a nursing mother may assume an upright position, head above water and tilted back, tusks parallel to the surface. Her calf then eagerly suckles as it clings to her vertically, half submerged and upside down, with its hindflippers flopping contentedly above water.

An Atlantic walrus mother nurses her calf. If disturbed, a mother will carry her offspring piggyback on her neck or even cradle it in her foreflippers as she swims to safety. FRED BRUEMMER

65

IN THE ANNALS OF

WALRUS LORE, A

WALRUS MOTHER'S

LOYALTY TO HER

CALF IS ALMOST

LEGENDARY.

The third and most crucial reason that the walrus birth rate is low is that a walrus cow is biologically programmed to give birth in alternate years, not annually. After winter mating, a cow's long pregnancy, lasting well over a year, dictates that her next act of parturition cannot occur until the second anniversary of her previous pup's birth. Thus, as a general rule, no more than half of all sexually mature females in a walrus population are likely to become pregnant, and no more than half are likely to give birth, during a given year.

How do biologists know that walruses have such long gestation periods? Most pinnipeds do. In addition, some elementary arithmetic provides valuable clues. The Pacific walrus calving season generally begins in about April and continues to about July, with most births taking place in May or June. Since mating occurs months earlier, in midwinter, the gestation period of walruses would have to be either improbably short (a mere few months) for such a large mammal, or, alternatively, it would have to be exceptionally long (well over a year).

The solution to this apparent paradox lies in a physiological phenomenon known as delayed implantation. In walruses, as in other sexually reproducing mammals, conception occurs at the instant a male's sperm fertilizes an egg cell, fusing the genetic content of these two parental germ cells, inside the uterus of a sexually mature female. But in walruses, as well as in certain other animal species, the fertilized egg cell does not quickly attach to the uterine wall to begin normal embryonic development into a fetus. Rather, it divides to form a microscopic, many-celled hollow sphere, known as a blastocyst, that floats freely in the cow's uterus for several months before attaching. As a result, a baby walrus conceived in, say, early March is not likely to continue normal embryonic development until sometime in June. Thus, this delay must be added to the normal period of embryonic growth in order to calculate the total gestation period for a pregnant walrus. The result: walrus calves are typically born a full fifteen months after conception.

In the annals of walrus lore, a walrus mother's loyalty to her calf is almost legendary. When the pair have hauled out on an ice floe, she rarely take her eyes off the young animal for long, and she may threaten, even viciously attack, any herd member that approaches her offspring too closely. Although mothers with very young calves tend to retreat to the relative calm of separate nursery herds, some calves inevitably die in the day-to-day crush within the main herds.

Early European hunters engaged in the wholesale slaughter of walruses, often baiting a mother with her injured calf and then quickly dispatching her with a bullet. Yet they sometimes seemed genuinely moved by her heroic attempts to rescue her wounded offspring, as can be seen in this ornate passage taken from the chronicles of a late-nineteenth-century Arctic voyage:

> When the fishermen chance to find them
> upon a flake of ice with their young ones,
> she casteth her young ones before her in the water,
> and then takes them in her arms
> and so plungeth up and down with them;
> and when shee will revenge herself upon the boates,
> or make resistance against them,
> then she cast her young ones from her again,
> and with all her force goeth toward the boat,
> thinking to overthrow it.

Alaskan wildlife biologist John J. Burns offers more contemporary confirmation of the strong bond between walrus mothers and their young. He reports that he has seen cows go to great lengths to retrieve and carry away dead or wounded calves after the young animals have been shot by hunters.

And on one memorable occasion, he watched a walrus cow rescue her calf after it had accidentally fallen into a deep crevasse. After ferociously rebuffing his attempts to assist her, she proceeded to flail away with her tusks at a massive chunk of ice that separated her from her offspring. Deploying her tusks as tandem ice axes, she eventually totally demolished the large ice block, ultimately freeing her trapped calf.

Social squabbles

Walruses rank among the most gregarious of all pinnipeds. They routinely congregate on ice or land in dense herds that may number in the many hundreds (or, in the case of Pacific walruses, many thousands) of animals. Like their huge, equally tactile southern cousins the elephant seals, they seem to prefer to lie in direct physical contact with, or at least close to, fellow herd members rather than alone, even when there is plenty of surplus haul-out space available.

In a walrus's world, the urge for such close contact almost certainly has its evolutionary rewards. For example, when winter temperatures plummet, huddling together on the ice presumably helps reduce each walrus's loss of body heat. And tightly packed herds are probably far more effective than loosely packed ones at instantly relaying a fellow herd member's alarm signals at the first sign of danger.

Most of a walrus's time on ice or land is spent lounging or sleeping. As they rest, herd members engage in sporadic bouts of shoving, bickering and squabbling, punctuated with an assortment of boisterous belches, snorts, coughs, growls and roars. Such interactions between herd members of both sexes and various ages serve to reinforce the social hierarchy of which each animal is a part. Some of a walrus's most socially revealing interactions take place whenever an individual animal exits the water, hauls out and rejoins a herd. For at such times, it must negotiate for a new resting space within the densely packed horde.

When it first encounters another animal in its path, the newly arrived walrus—male or female—typically tilts back its head and raises its tusks into a horizontal position, accentuating their size and condition. If necessary, the newcomer may also aggressively challenge other herd members adjacent to its path. It may, for example, feint or jab at them with its tusks, engage in a bluff charge or emphasize its lofty social rank with a series of belligerent roars. Sometimes, in its effort to cut a swathe through the toothsome crowd, it may even resort to scrambling right over the top of the prostrate bodies of dozing herd members. Once it has successfully run the gauntlet of poised tusks and vocal challenges, it can finally flop down on its own small patch of fetid ice, redolent of the fishy, ammoniated odours of nearby puddles of steaming walrus urine and feces.

A SEAFOOD SMORGASBORD

Walruses are voracious eaters. In fact, adults routinely wolf down between 50 and 85 kilograms (between 110 and 190 pounds) of marine invertebrates per day. But when it comes to selecting from the vast smorgasbord of seafood available to them on the ocean floor, it is clear they are also fairly finicky.

Forsaking swift-moving fish that are prized by some pinnipeds, walruses feed almost entirely on sluggish or virtually immobile bottom-dwelling, or benthic, shellfish. Judging, in part, by the stomach contents of numbers of dead walruses, the typical diet of a Pacific walrus includes favoured local varieties of clams, whelks, cockles and mussels. This basic diet is often seasonally supplemented by an assortment of other invertebrate species that flourish in the upper 10 to 20 centimetres (4 to 8 inches) of ocean floor sediments. Among them: various kinds of marine snails, worms, crabs and shrimp, as well as the occasional slow-moving fish or seabird.

Crucial details of walrus eating habits remain a mystery. Like so many of the

Occasionally, rogue walruses such as this one abandon their customary diet of marine invertebrates to prey exclusively on local seals. MATS FORSBERG

walrus's vital activities, feeding takes place under water, in frigid, poorly lit and often extremely remote settings. As a result, much information about walruses' feeding techniques tends to be largely anecdotal.

Not long ago, for example, many scientists assumed that a walrus's tusks played a key role in feeding. They were generally thought to function as picks or rakes, allowing the feeding animal to plow through muddy clam beds in pursuit of prey, leaving a characteristic trail of pits and furrows in its wake. Today this view is no longer widely held. The prevailing hypothesis is that walrus tusks serve a more passive role. A hungry walrus probably swims parallel to and just above the ocean floor, with only its muzzle and the convex outer surface of its paired tusks in direct contact with the sea bottom. Based on tusk abrasion patterns and other anatomical clues, it appears that the tusks probably act as sled runners, stabilizing—perhaps even protecting—the walrus's vulnerable head and mouth as the animal hovers over the fertile seafloor.

Like a blind person's white cane, a walrus's tusks may also provide valuable tactile clues as the animal swims in deep, sunless waters, mere centimetres above the seafloor. But even more subtle tactile signals may be triggered by the hundreds of long, bristly whiskers located on the walrus's muzzle. As a walrus cruises through the inky darkness of the Arctic seas, these stiff, quill-like appendages are thought to penetrate surface layers of sea-bottom ooze, where they serve as acutely sensitive sensory probes. Thus, even in low light and amid the muddy turbulence of the hunt, a bottom-feeding walrus can easily detect the hard outer contours of clams, snails and other solid objects embedded in the seafloor.

Walruses can also exert voluntary control over the movements of their whiskers, or vibrissae, using them almost as we use chopsticks. Anyone who has watched a captive walrus in a zoo knows that these animals can easily pick up and manipulate objects using their extended whiskers and the remarkably dexterous facial, or mustachial, pads to which these are anchored. And captive walruses are also astonishingly adept at squirting well-aimed jets of water from their mouths to move objects.

The stomach contents of dead walruses seldom contain shell fragments. The absence of such debris suggests that walruses do not eat clams and other shellfish whole, crushing them with their cheek teeth and then swallowing them shell and all. Rather, they appear to have mastered the fine art of devouring the tender meat of mollusks without having to ingest their outer armour.

How do walruses manage to carry out this nimble gastronomic feat? The secret, most biologists now believe, is suction. Studies of captive animals suggest that walruses can generate a sizable negative pressure, or vacuum force, in their narrow, high-roofed mouths, using a combination of quick inhalations of breath and pumping movements with their fleshy, pistonlike tongues.

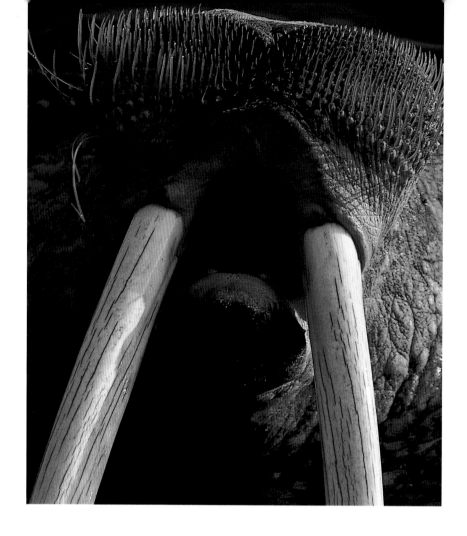

In sum, a walrus's mouth can be said to function somewhat like a high-powered vacuum cleaner, permitting the animal to neatly slice off the tasty feet, siphons and other soft body parts of, for example, clams and other bivalves. And, using such oral suction, in combination with deft manipulations of its mobile lips, mustachial pads and whiskers, it is probably able to harvest large quantities of the nutritious innards of such benthic marine invertebrates in rapid, almost assembly-line fashion, discarding inedible shell fragments in the process.

On rare occasions, certain adult male walruses sometimes display a sinister shift in food preference. Forsaking their usual diet of marine invertebrates, they develop a taste for the warm-blooded flesh of local pinnipeds, including, for example, bearded, ring or common seals. These rogue bulls feed largely on seal carrion, but they also

Walruses have been described as "vacuum cleaners of the sea." They have strong lips, narrow mouths and thick, pistonlike tongues that allow them to suck out the soft innards of clams, cockles and other shellfish without having to crush their shells. JEFF FOOTT

reportedly attack young animals, stabbing and then eviscerating their vulnerable prey with their sharp tusks. Biologist say that they can sometimes identify these predatory walruses by visible signs of such kills, including dark, telltale yellowish stains of seal blood and seal fat on their normally white tusks and pale hides.

The Perils of Predators

Besides gun-toting human hunters, few Arctic predators are big and fierce enough to routinely prey on walruses in the wild. For most would-be walrus predators, the risk of serious injury from the walruses' tusks is probably unacceptably high. For with its remarkable agility, slashing tusks, thick armour of skin and stupendous size, an agitated walrus does indeed constitute a formidable foe. Moreover, whole herds of angry walruses, including fiercely protective mothers with dependent young, have been known to aggressively turn on an intruder, human or nonhuman.

Out on the pack ice, polar bears do occasionally approach herds of basking walruses, sending them thundering into the sea. And Russian biologists suggest that during summer months polar bears do often kill significant numbers of young or injured herd members. But they are not usually effective predators of adult walruses. Thus, in most cases, if a polar bear is spotted gnawing on a dead walrus, the carcass is likely to be either a freshly killed young or injured animal or else the scavenged residue of a recent Native subsistence harvest.

At sea, marauding pods of killer whales can occasionally prove to be more than a match for a group of walruses. Fleeing walruses have been known to fling themselves out of the water and up on an ice floe in apparent terror, sometimes even crushing young calves in their path, to escape the jaws of pursuing orcas. As with polar bears, young walrus calves are usually the killer whale's primary target, although fully grown walruses do sometimes bear the scars of failed orca attacks.

WALRUSES CAN EXERT VOLUNTARY CONTROL OVER THE MOVEMENTS OF THEIR WHISKERS, OR VIBRISSAE, USING THEM ALMOST AS WE USE CHOPSTICKS.

In one case, a Russian observer recorded the details of a remarkably well-coordinated killer whale attack on a large congregation of swimming walruses. First, the pod of fifteen orcas circled the seventy or so wary walruses. Then suddenly two orcas split off from the rest of their group and swam right through a cluster of nervously milling walruses, in the process neatly separating a dozen or so of them from the rest like a pair of cowboys cutting cattle. Before long, the remaining killer whales joined the first pair in a final, brutal, slashing assault on this target group of isolated walruses, eventually leaving little more than ragged slabs of flesh and billowing clouds of blood in their wake.

*A lone Pacific walrus loafs on
a rocky Alaskan shore.* BRYAN
AND CHERRY ALEXANDER

HUNTERS AND

Part Three

WALRUSES

From the walrus [Native peoples of the North] obtained food and fuel, as well as materials for making tools, shelters, boats, sleds and clothing. In all probability, the harvesting of walruses by these indigenous peoples before the 18th century had little impact on the populations. The primitive hunter was not equipped to kill great numbers of these animals and had no incentive to take more than were required to meet his own daily needs.

—FRANCIS FAY, "The Ecology and Biology of the Pacific Walrus"

ANCIENT INUIT HUNTERS

For as long as human beings have inhabited circumpolar Arctic shores, whether in North America, Europe or Asia, or on adjacent islands, they have lived in intimate association with walruses and other pinnipeds and have expertly hunted them. Some coastal Arctic aboriginal groups, including the Netsilik Inuit, among others, traditionally relied almost entirely on marine mammals, and in particular, pinnipeds, including walruses, to sustain them.

Like caribou, foxes, belugas and other Arctic mammals, seals, sea lions and walruses were laden with astonishing gifts to enhance human survival in the North. Walruses have provided, for instance, meat, oil and hides, as well as tusks of dense, carvable ivory.

Consider just a few of the countless practical ways in which traditional Inuit

PAGES 76–77

A restless Pacific walrus bull clambers over the bodies of fellow herd members in search of a new resting spot.

ROBERT E. BARBER

79

and Eskimo society employed precious walrus body parts. Walrus meat and viscera provided nutritious food for both humans and sled dogs. Two female Pacific walrus hides could be sewed together to fashion a sturdy, flexible, waterproof covering for a 9-metre (30 foot) *umiak*, or skin boat. Calf hides could be braided into a light, strong, pliable leather rope used for harpoon lines. Thin, inflatable skin from the large, saclike pharyngeal pouches of bulls could be used as a membranous cover for drums. Blubber could be rendered into fuel oil to light stone lamps and cooking stoves. Intestines could be used to manufacture rain gear. And tusks could be carved into harpoon tips and an assortment of other weapons and tools.

Ancient Inuit and Eskimo myths include the walrus in their vivid accounts of the creation of sea mammals. One such narrative is the popular and geographically

Inuit artist Mathew Saviadjuk captures the rapierlike tusks and rippling body form of a fully grown walrus in a sculpture entitled Alert Walrus. PHOTOGRAPH BY KENJI NAGAI. REPRODUCED BY PERMISSION OF SPIRIT WRESTLER GALLERY, VANCOUVER, B.C.

widespread story of Sedna, a fierce matriarchal figure who serves as guardian of the entire marine fauna of northern seas.

In one version of this tale, Sedna is portrayed as an arrogant and romantic young girl who stubbornly refuses to marry. She is unwittingly seduced by a fierce predatory seabird, a northern fulmar who is masquerading as a handsome young man. Smitten by her new suitor, she flees the village of her furious father to take up residence with the young man in a faraway land, only to discover later that she has been deceived.

When Sedna's father learns of the humanoid seabird's clever deception, he boldly attempts to rescue her by boat. But just as the two are making their escape, the returning fulmar spots them from overhead and, in a rage, whips up the seas with furious beatings of his wings.

In a panic, Sedna's cruel father throws his young daughter overboard, hoping to lighten his load and perhaps calm the inflamed passions of her angry lover. In a final act of betrayal, as his drowning daughter clings desperately to the gunwales of his boat, he proceeds to abandon her by ruthlessly chopping off her fingers, one segment at a time, with a series of blows.

The mutilated fragments of Sedna's fingers fall into the storm-tossed sea, where they are instantly transformed into primordial sea mammals. The first segments to hit the water's surface turn into small seals. The next ones become bearded seals. And the last, and largest in diameter, turn into fat, wrinkled walruses.

Tragically, poor Sedna drowns. Her body slowly sinks to the dark ocean floor, where she is reborn to live eternally as the powerful Mother of Sea Beasts. Her divine task is to forever mete out harsh justice on behalf of all marine life each time an Inuit hunter, or other human being, acts in a way that upsets the sacred balance of nature.

Ever since her descent, it has been the responsibility of the traditional Inuit *angakoq*, or shaman, to periodically pay Sedna a visit. Deep in a trance, the *angakoq* is first required to enter the spirit of a walrus or another local marine mammal.

Inuit hunters, harpoons in hand, wait patiently for an unsuspecting walrus to surface. Today, in certain parts of the world, Native subsistence hunting remains a significant factor in walrus mortality. Properly managed, it also has the potential to nourish Native communities in both body and soul. BRYAN AND CHERRY ALEXANDER

Then he makes the perilous journey down to her dim, undersea abode, where he earnestly pleads with her to release generations of seals, sea lions and walruses yet to be born so that Inuit people can continue to survive.

Traditional Inuit and Eskimo hunters routinely paid homage to the potent spirit of Sedna, as revealed in the following passage from a Netsilik seal-hunting song addressed to Sedna, or Nuliajuk:

> You sweet orphan Nuliajuk,
> I beg you now
> bring me a gift,
> not anything from the land
> but a gift from the sea,
> something that will make a nice soup.
> Dare I say it right out?
> I want a seal!

Even with Sedna's divine assistance in ensuring a perpetual abundance of marine life in Arctic waters, the traditional Inuit hunter faced formidable challenges in trying to daily track, stalk and kill local sea mammals. Indeed, the amphibious habits of seals, sea lions and walruses often posed special problems for the Native hunter.

True, pinnipeds are generally rather clumsy on land, making them vulnerable to hunters. But their almost uncanny ability to rapidly flee into nearby bodies of water means that hunters had to devise clever strategies for approaching and slaying them as well as for quickly retrieving their carcasses before they sank out of sight.

Ancient Inuit techniques for hunting walruses are testimony to the Inuit hunter's

ingenuity. The two principal weapons for hunting walruses, as well as other marine mammal species, were the skin-covered boat and the harpoon. The sleek, single-passenger kayak, along with its much larger multipassenger cousin the *umiak*, offered the Native hunter an unparalleled combination of stealth and mobility during the often long and gruelling ocean voyages to traditional hauling grounds on remote ice fields, islands or shores. Moreover, such vessels allowed the hunter not only to approach his quarry from the sea but also to retrieve a dead animal, secure it and transport it safely back home.

The intricate Inuit harpoon greatly facilitated the kill, for it granted the hunter the ability to strike large sea mammals from a relatively safe distance while remaining securely tethered to his extremely mobile prey. The Inuit harpoon is, in essence, a

Walrus Surprises Hunter *by Inuit artist Napachie Pootoogook*. COURTESY OF W. BAFFIN ESKIMO COOPERATIVE.

modified spear, and it appears in a variety of subtly modified forms throughout Inuit cultures. A typical kayak harpoon, for example, is equipped with a large, jointed spearhead fashioned from a walrus tusk, which is capped with a detachable ivory tip.

When a hunter threw or thrust the harpoon at a walrus, the razor-sharp tip, attached by a line to an inflated sealskin, pierced the walrus's thick hide and remained lodged there after the spear's long wooden shaft had fallen or drifted away. And when the wounded animal attempted to swim away, it was forced to struggle against the buoyant force of the sealskin float still firmly attached to the ivory tip embedded in its flesh. Eventually, the hunter paddled out in his kayak to pick up the float, reel in the dying beast and finally dispatch it with a sharp lance or crushing blows to the head.

Some faint sense of the ancient drama of the Inuit walrus can be gleaned from this traditional walrus hunting song, composed by an Inuit shaman named Aua and recorded by the Danish ethnographer Knud Rasmussen in his book *Across the Arctic*, first published in 1927:

> I could not sleep
> For the sea was so smooth
> Near at hand.
> So I rowed out
> And up came a walrus
> Close by my kayak.
> It was too near to throw,
> So I thrust my harpoon into its side
> And the bladder-float danced across the waves.

Early European hunters

Although the archaeological record is sparse, there is some evidence that Stone Age European hunters also seasonally hunted a variety of sea mammals. Ancient coast dwellers, living in what is now France, Denmark and Scandinavia, left behind drawings depicting gray seals, harp seals and other local pinnipeds. And they almost certainly hunted walruses on occasion.

Like Inuit myths, early European folklore also gave a spiritual dimension to the walrus, which once ranged along the continent's northernmost shores. But, in time, European society came to look upon walruses almost exclusively in economic terms.

Beginning in the ninth century, enterprising Vikings, followed later by other northern Europeans, relentlessly pursued the *hvalross,* or whale horse, in its icy retreats off the coast of Greenland and elsewhere. They eagerly slaughtered entire herds of animals on their crowded hauling grounds in order to obtain valuable ivory tusks, as well as blubber, hides and other commercially useful by-products.

The primacy of such profit motives, even in very early European walrus hunts, is apparent in this brief statement by a ninth-century Norse voyager named Othere, in his report to Alfred the Great about a recent expedition to the White Sea. He states that he "chiefly went thither, in addition to the seeing of the country, on account of the horse-whale [walrus] because they have very good bone in their teeth; and their hides are very good for ships' ropes."

In Greenland, beginning as early as the tenth century, Norse colonists actively traded walrus and narwhal ivory in exchange for essential European goods. And for much of the past three or centuries or so, British, Norwegian and Russian hunters have relentlessly hunted walruses in the more accessible areas of their original range in northeastern Atlantic waters.

Throughout the Middle Ages, a lucrative international trade in tusks provided wealthy Europeans with a steady flow of raw walrus ivory. It often served as a form of currency or else was fashioned into a variety of luxury art objects, ranging from intricate carvings to elaborate chess sets. The lure of quick profits proved deadly to the walrus. It soon led to severe overharvesting, eventually eradicating the walrus population from the European continent and imperilling vulnerable walrus populations in other parts of the species' once vast range.

COMMERCIAL WALRUS HUNTING

It is tempting to romanticize the ancient bond between traditional Native hunters and marine mammals. Nonetheless, before the arrival of Europeans in North America, the ecological effect of small, scattered Inuit hunting communities on primal Arctic walrus populations, probably numbering in the tens of millions of animals, must have been slight.

But in the wake of the arrival of the first waves of European newcomers to the New World, the relationship between hunters and walruses underwent a profound transformation. By the sixteenth century, as Basque fleets began to fish the cod stocks on the Grand Banks off the coast of Newfoundland, change was already in the wind. At that time, large numbers of walruses still ranged as far south as, for example, Sable Island, off Nova Scotia, and the Magdalen Islands, in the Gulf of St. Lawrence. And visiting fishermen, whose northern European neighbours back home had already hunted walruses and traded in walrus ivory for centuries, could not help but take notice of the great herds of hauled-out walruses (not to mention harp seals and other sea mammals) in the vicinity.

Soaring prices for whale oil on European markets soon provided a powerful incentive for large-scale commercial whaling operations. Pinniped blubber, it turned out, also contained valuable oil. Thus, it quickly became common practice for profit-seeking European whaling ships to top up their whale-oil cargo with oil

AT THE HEIGHT OF THE EUROPEAN COMMERCIAL TRADE, WALRUS HIDE FOUND ITS WAY INTO A LONG LIST OF MANUFACTURED PRODUCTS, RANGING FROM GLUE, CARRIAGE TRACES AND LUGGAGE TO INDUSTRIAL BUFFING WHEELS, AUTOMOBILE TIRES AND POOL CUE TIPS.

Commercial walrus hunters
slaughtered the walrus for its
oil-laden blubber, as well as
for its tusks and hide.
MATS FORSBERG

93

obtained from sea lions or walruses. As a result, most sealing activities tended to be intimately associated with those of commercial whaling. And as European colonists continued to settle eastern coastal regions of North America over the ensuing centuries, a rising demand for walrus tusks, hides and oil-laden blubber often paralleled the demand for whale products.

It did not take long for the impact of commercial European walrus harvesting in North America to eclipse that of early Native subsistence hunting. Not surprisingly, many northern Native communities were soon swept up and fundamentally transformed by these and other intrusive economic forces. For example, as the trade networks of the Hudson's Bay Company and other enterprises began to reach even the most remote Arctic aboriginal communities, local Inuit hunters came under enormous economic pressure to abandon their traditional reverence and restraint towards walruses and other important game animals. In exchange, of course, they would be rewarded with unprecedented material gains.

Many Native hunters soon succumbed to the lure of European markets. By selling products from wildlife that they had once procured strictly for subsistence or regional trade, they could soon purchase firearms and other useful imported products. Such tools enabled increasing numbers of Inuit hunters to kill walruses, as well as other commercially valuable game animals, with ruthless efficiency, in time threatening the very foundations of ancient Native values and cosmologies.

European walrus hunters relied, in large measure, on very similar equipment. But commercial sealing operations tended to be carried out on a far grander scale. By the eighteenth century, for example, many sealers were equipped not just with modern firearms but also with specially designed harpoons, lances and boats that enabled them to conduct harvests that were even more lethally efficient. In addition, large numbers of walruses were killed in nocturnal raids on their hauling grounds, using a combination of hand-held lances and teams of trained attack dogs.

Commercial sealers of this era tended to use the same basic gear used by contemporary whalers—sharp flensing knives, cast-iron boiling pots, wooden storage barrels—to render thick strips of walrus blubber into oil. They also harvested the thick, durable hides that ancient European warriors had once employed for manufacturing battle shields. And during the period of the European commercial trade, walrus hide found its way into a long list of manufactured products, ranging from glue, carriage traces and luggage to industrial buffing wheels, automobile tires and pool cue tips.

THE CONSEQUENCES OF COMMERCIAL HARVESTS

In time, in the sealing industry, as in the whaling industry, commercial profiteering gradually destroyed the very wildlife populations on which it depended. As a result, today, in some parts of the world, particularly in more accessible Atlantic regions, walrus populations have really never fully recovered from centuries of persistent overharvesting.

By the mid-nineteenth century, for example, European sealers had all but destroyed once plentiful walrus populations in the eastern Atlantic in places such as Bear Island and Svalbard. And during the first decades of the twentieth century, aided by modern power boats and other equipment, sealers gradually extended the reach of their harvests to such distant walrus population centres as Franz Josef Land, a remote Arctic archipelago lying off the northern coast of Russia.

Partly because it was often closer to large human populations, the Atlantic walrus suffered far greater losses from centuries of human exploitation than did its more geographically isolated Pacific cousin. In the western Atlantic, for example, walruses historically ranged along the coast of eastern Canada as far south as Nova

Scotia and the Gulf of St. Lawrence (where, in 1534, an awestruck Jacques Cartier first spotted hordes of the great sea beasts off Brions Island that looked to him "like large oxen," with enormous tusks "like elephants'"). Today walruses are rarely sighted as far south as Labrador. And in eastern Atlantic waters, although they were once occasionally encountered as far south as Scotland and the Hebrides (one was reportedly taken in the River Thames in England in 1456), they no longer inhabit the continental coast of northern Europe.

In the western Atlantic region, commercial sealers seriously depleted walrus populations well into the twentieth century—in the eastern Canadian Arctic, around Baffin Bay and Davis Strait, for instance, as well as off the coast of Greenland, among other locations. As recently as 1951, a Norwegian sealing expedition reportedly killed more than twelve hundred animals in one of the last known major commercial walrus hunts in the Davis Inlet area. And sealers killed an estimated twelve thousand walruses off the western coast of Greenland between 1900 and 1978.

In the Pacific region, the history of walrus hunting followed a somewhat different course. Large-scale commercial harvesting of Pacific walruses did not commence in the Bering Sea region until about the middle of the eighteenth century, fuelled largely by an insatiable Russian demand for ivory. During the first century or so of its operations, the Russian sealing industry also magnified its damage to Pacific walrus stocks by specifically targeting sexually mature bulls, either slaughtering them directly for their bounty of ivory or else bartering for the big tusks with local Native communities.

The effect of such commercial harvests was often devastating. In the Bering Sea's remote Pribilof Islands, for instance, large numbers of Pacific walruses had historically frequented shores not far from those of the breeding rookeries of the famous Pribilof fur seal. But during a single year of sealing the Russian American Company, for example, reportedly harvested some 12,700 kilograms (28,000 pounds)

of ivory from mixed herds of walruses, equal to the ivory contained in the tusks of three thousand full-grown bulls. Faced with such fearsome hunting pressures, those walruses that did survive the commercial hunt eventually abandoned their traditional local haunts, with the result that today walruses are rarely encountered here.

By the mid-nineteenth century, American whalers, in pursuit of commercially valuable bowhead whales in western Arctic waters, were also taking huge numbers of Pacific walruses. For example, according to some estimates, U.S. expeditions in this region harvested at least 140,000 animals between 1848 and 1914 alone. Because sealers often killed males and females indiscriminately, the long-term effect of commercial hunting on Pacific walrus populations, with their male-centred polygynous breeding systems and ponderously slow reproductive rates, was often profound.

MODERN NATIVE SUBSISTENCE HUNTING

In 1941, the United States finally outlawed commercial walrus harvests, as Canada had done in 1931, with the exception, in both countries, of limited, officially sanctioned Native subsistence hunts. Authorized Native hunts were intended to allow Native communities to continue to harvest limited numbers of walruses each year to meet local dietary, craft and artistic needs, as many of the communities have done since time immemorial.

However admirable this aim, the original ideals of Native subsistence hunting of walruses have, in some cases, been seriously compromised as modern economic pressures have increasingly superseded traditional subsistence needs. In the United States, for example, Native subsistence hunting of walruses tends to be largely unregulated, with no officially designated seasons, bag limits, or sex or age restrictions. So it is hardly surprising that some Native communities end up

FACING PAGE
A wary walrus soaks in the shallows.
THOMAS KITCHIN

harvesting far more walruses per capita then they could possibly consume for ordinary "subsistence" purposes.

In principle, raw, uncarved walrus tusks obtained in Native subsistence hunts cannot be exported, and their use is restricted to legitimate Native artisans and craftspeople. But there is always a temptation to plunder local walrus populations for short-term personal gain. Sadly, the lure of quick profits on the international black market for walrus and elephant ivory has seduced a small number of poachers into wantonly slaughtering substantial numbers of walruses solely for their valuable tusks. The great beasts are simply shot and beheaded, their fresh, steaming carcasses left out on the ice to rot. According to recent reports, as many as five hundred headless walrus carcasses now wash ashore each year in coastal western Alaska alone. And they are surely only the tip of the proverbial iceberg.

Even perfectly legitimate Native walrus hunts can prove exceedingly wasteful. Recent studies have shown, for example, that at least half of all walruses shot by hunters—Native and non-Native alike—are never successfully retrieved. As sometimes happened to the unsuccessful traditional Inuit hunter, the wounded animal often manages to flee into the water, where it drowns. And before the hunter can reach the walrus and properly secure it, it often sinks like a stone.

In recent decades, Native peoples in a number of polar nations throughout the world have continued to hunt walruses with high-powered rifles. In the past, a few thousand walruses have been killed annually in the state of Alaska, with the largest Eskimo harvests taking placing not far from the Bering Strait, in villages such as Gambell, King Island and Little Diomede Island. And during the 1970s and 1980s, the Canadian catch reportedly averaged slightly over five hundred animals per year.

Substantially smaller Native walrus harvests, with annual kills generally numbering in the hundreds of animals, still take place in Siberia, Greenland's

OF HEAVY METAL

CONTAMINANTS AND

ORGANOCHLORINE

PESTICIDE RESIDUES,

AMONG OTHER

TOXINS, ARISING FROM

HUMAN ACTIVITIES.

Thule district and elsewhere. But there is a distinct possibility, according to some experts, that these hunts could decline or even disappear altogether as gasoline-powered snowmobiles continue to replace ravenous sled dogs that eat walrus meat.

Today Native subsistence hunters are said to be responsible for most recorded Pacific walrus mortality. But they are hardly the only parties to have hunted Pacific walruses during the latter half of the twentieth century. Soviet sealers, for instance, reportedly slaughtered up to eight thousand Pacific walruses a year during the three decades ending in 1960. For a time, in the 1980s, they resumed their commercial walrus hunts, including limited, officially sanctioned harvests conducted from ships operating in both the Chukchi and Bering Seas. But with the collapse of the Soviet Union, commercial walrus hunting in Russia has apparently been all but abandoned. Commercial fox farms that once relied on walrus meat as a food source are gone. The northern sealing fleet lies rusting and in disrepair. And a state-controlled ivory artifact industry has disappeared.

Even though large-scale commercial hunting of walruses has dramatically declined during this century, other, more insidious threats to the world's walrus populations are on the rise. One such threat is marine pollution. The fat tissues of a number of pinniped species around the globe have already begun to reveal worrisome levels of heavy metal contaminants and organochlorine pesticide residues, among other toxins, arising from human activities.

Fortunately, preliminary studies of such toxins in certain walrus populations suggest that walruses may actually be faring slightly better than many of their pinniped kin living closer to large-scale human settlements or industrial processes. Nonetheless, recent research in Alaskan waters has revealed sufficiently high levels of cadmium and mercury in the kidneys and livers of walruses to be potentially

A walrus's ivory tusks serve as weapons that help reinforce a social hierarchy of which each animal is a part. But they are also a precious commodity that can lure legitimate and illegitimate hunter alike.

TOM AND PAT LEESON

102

hazardous to walrus health and well-being, if not yet definitively hazardous to the Alaskan Native communities that harvest and consume walruses.

A host of other potent, often only partially understood forces, ranging from global warming, atmospheric ozone depletion and shifting ocean currents to burgeoning ecotourism are also potential threats to the long-term well-being of wild walruses. So, in the years ahead, it is vital that we vigilantly monitor the effects of such processes on behalf of walruses, as well as other Arctic species.

THE STATE OF THE WORLD'S WALRUSES

Today no accurate census exists for the world's far-flung walrus populations. But despite historic elimination of Atlantic walrus populations from portions of its original range, the news is clearly not all bad.

Today the Pacific subspecies of walrus probably constitutes between 80 and 90 per cent of the world's total population of walruses. After enduring at least three massive declines from overharvesting since the mid-nineteenth century, Pacific walrus populations have recently enjoyed several decades of recovery, reportedly doubling between 1960 and 1980 alone. By 1990, the total Pacific walrus population was estimated at over 200,000 animals. Some sources suggest, however, that this figure may have recently declined slightly, partly as a result of increased hunting during the 1980s, when, for a time, Alaska and the Soviet Union together killed up to 10,000 animals a year.

The Pacific walrus, in contrast to its Atlantic counterpart, has had several important factors in its favour. From the time of first human contact, the Pacific walrus was probably blessed with a huge population. In addition, large-scale commercial sealing did not reach the Pacific region until relatively recently. And during the height of commercial harvests, these animals were often able to retreat to exceedingly remote Arctic ice fields in the Chukchi and Bering Seas, beyond the reach of all but the most determined commercial sealer.

But bad news also abounds. Foremost is the simple fact that the beleaguered Atlantic walrus, which has been under relentless human assault for many centuries, has simply not enjoyed a comparable rebound in population. Unlike the rapidly recovering Pacific walrus, it has repeatedly failed to even begin to recolonize many critical areas of its historic range.

Despite hunting restrictions and other local conservation measures, recent estimates put the number of walruses in the northeastern Atlantic, for instance, at a paltry fifteen hundred to two thousand animals. Several thousand Atlantic walruses continue to frequent areas of the eastern Canadian Arctic, such as northern Hudson Bay, Foxe Basin, Davis Strait and Baffin Bay. And smaller numbers of walruses still survive off the coast of Greenland and elsewhere.

A PLACE FOR THE WALRUS

A herd of fitfully dozing walruses out on an Alaskan ice floe is suddenly disturbed. Alarmed, herd members rush headlong into the nearby sea in a noisy stampede, leaving roostertails of white ocean spray in their wake. Soon numbers of walruses resurface to explosively exhale in near unison. Some animals raise their blunt, tusk-burdened heads high above the water in an attempt to catch a glimpse of an intruder. Then they inhale, plunge back beneath the protective waves and are gone.

We are, in many ways, achingly ignorant about walruses. Yet this much seems reasonably clear: the ways of wild walruses appear to be fundamentally incompatible with persistent human disturbance, whether from unregulated commercial harvests, permanent human settlements, or major military, mining, oil drilling or other industrial operations in the Arctic. For historically, walruses, unlike some of their

A huge Pacific walrus

lolls in the Alaskan surf.

GUNTHER MATSCHKE

less sensitive pinniped kin, have repeatedly abandoned favoured traditional hauling grounds in the face of such pressures.

Yet who among us can deny that the walrus, by virtue of tens of millions of years of its own turbulent—and up to this point successful—evolutionary trials, earned a legitimate place in Arctic ecosystems long before naked *Homo sapiens* ever appeared on the scene?

As we have seen, however, the bond between humans and walruses has, with notable exceptions, been mostly troubled from the start. If, in the twenty-first century, we intend to honour what many of us view as the walrus's inherent right to exist—if we are truly willing to share the earth's vast northern seas and shores—then we must make sure that these wondrous creatures will always have access to the same relatively pristine Arctic waterways, islands and ice floes that have sustained their seasonal wanderings until now.

And perhaps, in the process, many more of us will have the opportunity to catch a glimpse of the inner beauty and grace that reside in the bloodshot eyes, ivory fangs, blubbery body and rumpled hide of one of nature's most widely mocked and misunderstood—yet beloved—beasts.

SELECTED REFERENCES

FACING PAGE

*Despite its small head,
bristly whiskers and rumpled
skin, perhaps we can begin
to appreciate the inner
beauty of the walrus.*

WAYNE LYNCH

Allen, Joel A. 1880. "History of North American Pinnipeds." Misc. Pub. No. 12. Washington, D.C.: Dept. of the Interior.

Boas, Franz. 1964. *The Central Eskimo*. Lincoln: University of Nebraska Press.

Bonner, W. Nigel. 1980. *The Natural History of Seals*. New York: Facts on File.

Brooks, J. W. 1954. "Life History and Ecology of the Pacific Walrus." Report No. 1. Fairbanks: Alaska Coop. Wildlife Unit.

Bruemmer, Fred. 1977. "The Gregarious but Contentious Walrus." *Natural History* 86 (9): 52–61.

Burns, J. J. 1965. *The Walrus in Alaska*. Juneau: Alaska Dept. of Fish and Game.

Carroll, Lewis. 1872. *Through the Looking Glass, and What Alice Found There*. (Illustrations by John Tenniel.) Boston: Lee and Shepard; New York: Lee, Shepard, and Dillingham.

Fay, Francis H. 1955. "The Pacific Walrus: Spatial Ecology, Life History, and Population." Ph.D. diss., University of British Columbia.

———. 1982. "The Ecology and Biology of the Pacific Walrus." North American Fauna Series No. 74. Washington, D.C.: U.S. Dept. of the Interior, Fish and Wildlife Service.

Godwin, Sara. 1990. *Seals*. New York: Mallard Press.

Kenyon, Karl. 1960. "The Pacific Walrus." *Oryx* 5 (6): 332–40.

King, Judith. 1983. *Seals of the World*. Ithaca, N.Y.: Comstock Pub. Associates.

McGhee, Robert. 1996. *Ancient People of the Arctic*. Vancouver: University of British Columbia Press.

Mansfield, T.H. 1958. "Biology of the Atlantic Walrus in the Eastern Canadian Arctic." Report No. 653. Ottawa: Fisheries Research Board of Canada.

———. 1966. "The Walrus in Canada's Arctic." *Canadian Geographic Journal* 72 (3): 88–95.

Miller, Edward H. 1975. "Walrus Ethology I: The Social Role of Tusks and Applications of Multidimensional Scaling." *Canadian Journal of Zoology* 53 (5): 590–613.

———. 1976. "Walrus Ethology II: Herd Structure and Activity Budget of Summering Males." *Canadian Journal of Zoology* 54 (5): 704–715.

Perry, Richard. 1967. *The World of the Walrus.* London: Cassell & Co.

Rasmussen, Knud. 1969. *Across Arctic America.* New York: Greenwood Press.

———. 1930. *Intellectual Culture of the Hudson Bay Eskimos.* Vol. VIII of *Report of the Fifth Thule Expedition, 1921-24.* Copenhagen: Gyldendal.

Reeves, Randall, Brent Stewart, and Stephen Leatherwood. 1992. *The Sierra Club Handbook of Seals and Sirenians.* San Francisco: Sierra Club Books.

Ridgway, Sam H., ed. 1972. *Mammals of the Sea, Biology and Medicine.* Springfield, Ill.: Charles C. Thompson.

Riedman, Marianne. 1990. *The Pinnipeds: Seals, Sea Lions, and Walruses.* Los Angeles: University of California Press.

Scheffer, Victor B. 1958. *Seals, Sea Lions, and Walruses: A Review of the Pinnipedia.* Stanford, Calif.: Stanford University Press.

Seidelman, Harold, and James Turner. 1993. *The Inuit Imagination.* Vancouver: Douglas & McIntyre.

INDEX